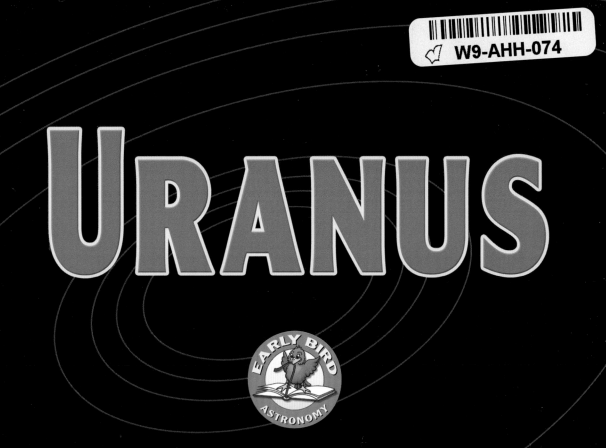

URANUS

BY GREGORY L. VOGT

LERNER PUBLICATIONS COMPANY • MINNEAPOLIS

The photographs in this book are used with permission of: NASA/CXC/SAO, p. 4; © Friedrich Saurer/Photo Researchers, Inc., p. 5; © Hulton Archive/Getty Images, pp. 6, 8; © Jack Guez/ AFP/Getty Images, p. 7; © Science Museum/Science & Society Picture Library/The Image Works, p. 9; © Bildarchiv Preussischer Kulturbesitz/Art Resource, NY, p. 10; ESO, p. 11; © Laura Westlund/Independent Picture Service, pp. 12-13, 16, 17, 25; The International Astronomical Union/Martin Kornmesser, p. 14; Lunar and Planetary Institute/NASA, p. 15; © Mark Garlick/Photo Researchers, Inc., pp. 18, 19, 34; © JPL/NASA/Time & Life Pictures/Getty Images, p. 20; © NASA/Time & Life Pictures/Getty Images, pp. 21, 23, 38 (right), 39, 40, 41; NASA/JPL/USGS, p. 22; © Silvio Verrecchia/Shuterstock Images, p. 24; © Ron Miller, p. 26; © Jason Reed/Photodisc/Getty Images, p. 27; Courtesy of Doug Mink, p. 28; Photos by Doug Mink, pp. 29, 30; Courtesy of de Pater, Hammel, Gibbard, and Showalter, p. 31; © Space Frontiers/Hulton Archive/Getty Images, p. 32; NASA/JPL, pp. 33 (top), 38 (left), 46; NASA/JPL/ STScI, p. 33 (bottom); © Science Source/Photo Researchers, Inc., p. 35; © Julian Baum/Photo Researchers, Inc., p. 36; NASA, pp. 37, 48 (bottom); © John Chumack/Photo Researchers, Inc., p. 42; © Detlev van Ravenswaay/Photo Researchers, Inc., p. 43; © Mauritius/SuperStock, p. 47; NASA, ESA and M. Showalter (SETI Institute), p. 48 (top).

Front cover: NASA/JPL/STScI.
Back cover: NASA, ESA, and the Hubble Heritage Team (STScI/AURA).

Lerner Publications Company
A division of Lerner Publishing Group, Inc.
241 First Avenue North
Minneapolis, MN 55401 U.S.A.

Website address: www.lernerbooks.com

Library of Congress Cataloging-in-Publication Data

Vogt, Gregory.
    Uranus / by Gregory L. Vogt.
       p.   cm. — (Early bird astronomy)
    Includes index.
    ISBN 978-0-7613-4156-7 (lib. bdg. : alk. paper)
    1. Uranus (Planet)—Juvenile literature. I. Title.
QB681.V643 2010
523.47—dc22   2008045299

Manufactured in the United States of America
1 2 3 4 5 6 – BP – 15 14 13 12 11 10

CONTENTS

BE A WORD DETECTIVE

Can you find these words as you read about Uranus?
Be a detective and try to figure out what they mean.
You can turn to the glossary on page 46 for help.

astronomers	moons	solar system
atmosphere	orbit	spacecraft
axis	rings	telescope
elliptical	rotate	

A Greek man named Hipparchus studied the skies long ago. How many planets could he see in the night sky?

CHAPTER 1
DISCOVERY!

For thousands of years, people have watched the planets. Long ago, people only knew of five planets besides Earth. Those planets were Mercury, Venus, Mars, Jupiter, and Saturn.

The planets looked like bright stars. But they were different from the stars. Each night, stars rise and set in the sky. The planets follow their own paths. The word *planet* comes from an old Greek word meaning "wanderer." People thought of the planets as wandering stars.

The planets Jupiter (LEFT) and Venus (RIGHT) shine like stars above the Moon (BELOW) in the night sky.

The telescope (TEH-luh-skohp) was invented in the early 1600s. People used telescopes to learn more about the stars and planets. Scientists called astronomers (uh-STRAH-nuh-muhrs) began to study the planets. They learned that Saturn had rings. Jupiter had stripes and tiny moons. Mars had light and dark shadows.

Galileo Galilei was a famous astronomer of the early 1600s. He built his own telescope in 1609 and used it to study Jupiter and Venus.

Astronomer Friedrich Wilhelm Herschel made this telescope for his sister, Caroline, who was also an astronomer. He used a similar telescope to discover a new planet.

In 1781 astronomer Friedrich Wilhelm Herschel made a discovery. Herschel had built his own telescope. With that telescope, he found a wandering star. It was very faint. It looked like a tiny blue green dot.

Herschel watched the dot as the wandering star traveled around the Sun beyond Saturn. Herschel knew that he had found another planet.

This painting shows stars dancing around Uranus, the Greek god of the sky. A German artist painted the scene in the early 1800s.

Herschel named the planet Georgium Sidus. Most of the other planets are named after ancient gods and goddesses. Herschel's planet was later renamed Uranus (YUR-uh-nuhs). In ancient Greece, Uranus was the god of the sky.

Astronomers have learned much more about Uranus since its discovery. They learned that it is made of gas, ice, and rock. It is four times bigger than Earth. And Uranus has many rings and moons.

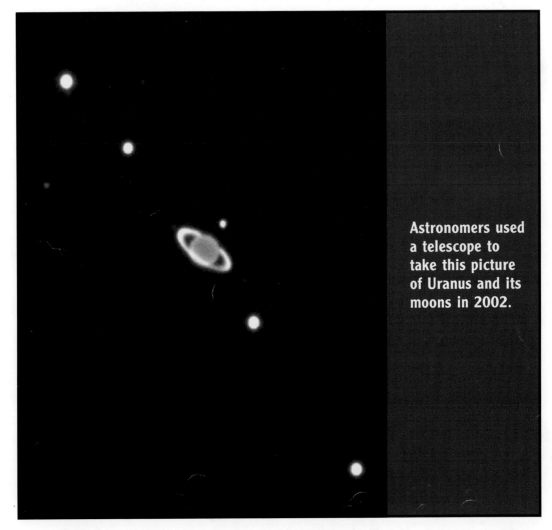

Astronomers used a telescope to take this picture of Uranus and its moons in 2002.

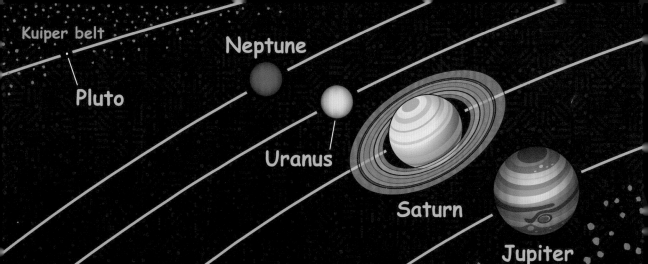

Kuiper belt

Neptune

Pluto

Uranus

Saturn

Jupiter

CHAPTER 2

SIDEWAYS PLANET

Uranus and Earth share the same neighborhood in space. They are both a part of the solar system. The solar system includes the Sun and eight planets. Dwarf planets and other objects are also part of the solar system. Dwarf planets are smaller than the eight main planets.

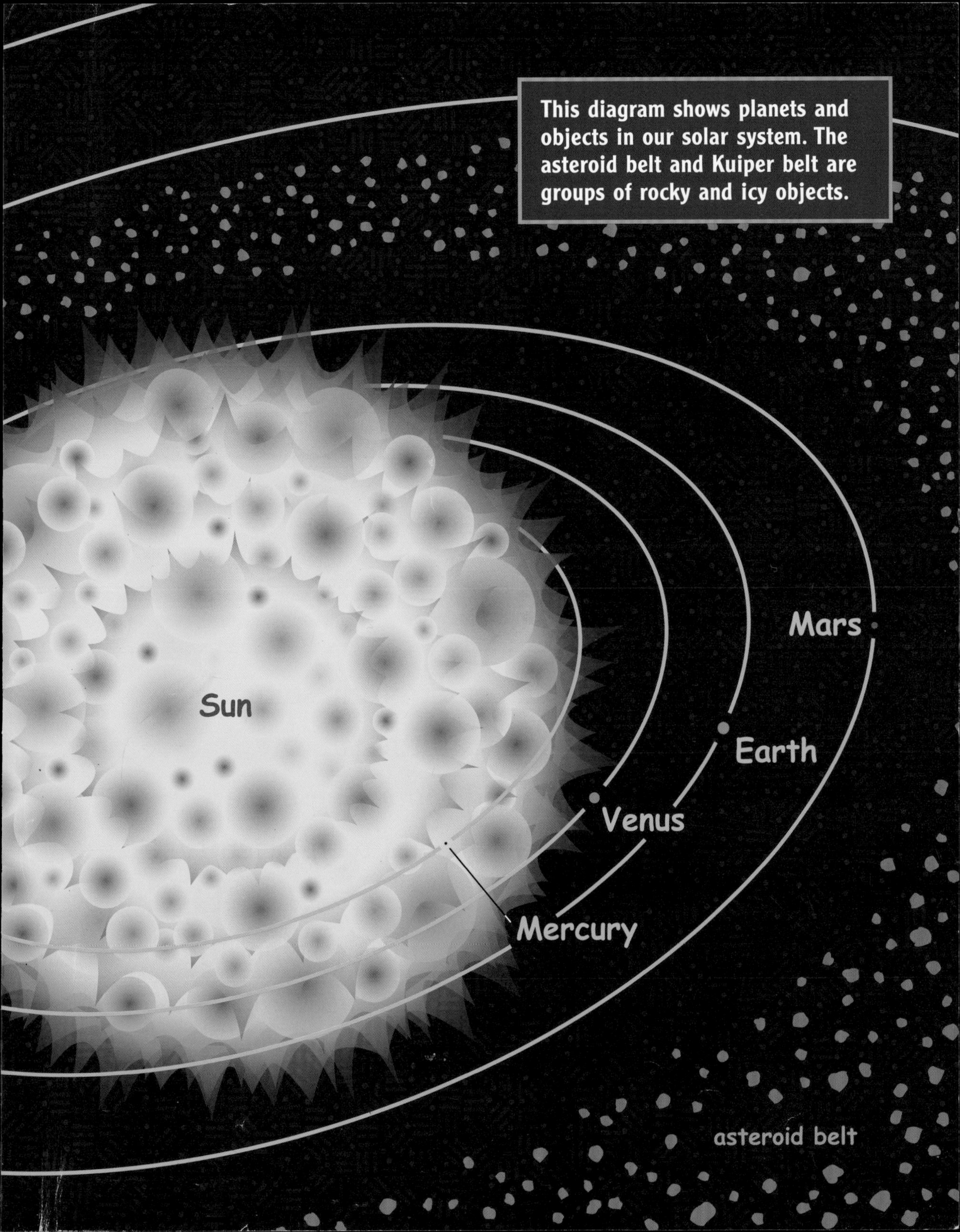

This diagram shows planets and objects in our solar system. The asteroid belt and Kuiper belt are groups of rocky and icy objects.

Mars

Earth

Sun

Venus

Mercury

asteroid belt

This picture shows the Sun (LEFT) and the eight planets of our solar system in order. The dwarf planet Pluto is at the far right.

The Sun lies at the center of the solar system. The planets closest to the Sun are Mercury, Venus, Earth, and Mars. These four planets are mostly made of solid rock. Scientists call them the rocky planets.

Jupiter, Saturn, Uranus, and Neptune are called gas giants. They are made mostly of gas. They are the largest planets in the solar system, and they are the farthest from the Sun.

Uranus is the third-largest planet. It measures 32,000 miles (50,000 kilometers) across. Only Jupiter and Saturn are larger.

Uranus is the seventh planet from the Sun. It is 1.8 billion miles (2.9 billion km) away from the Sun.

Jupiter (LEFT) and Saturn (CENTER) are the only planets bigger than Uranus (RIGHT). As these pictures show, Jupiter and Saturn are much bigger than Uranus.

The planets move through space around the Sun. Each planet follows its own path. That path is called an orbit. Uranus's orbit does not form a perfect circle around the Sun. Its orbit is shaped like an egg. Scientists call this shape elliptical (ih-LIHP-tih-cuhl).

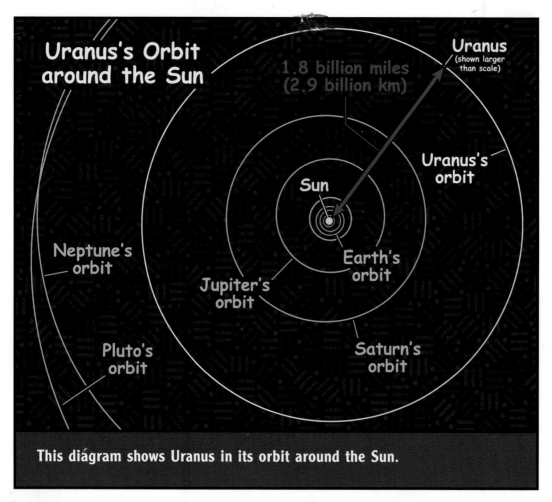

Uranus's Orbit around the Sun

1.8 billion miles (2.9 billion km)

Uranus (shown larger than scale)

Uranus's orbit

Sun

Neptune's orbit

Earth's orbit

Jupiter's orbit

Pluto's orbit

Saturn's orbit

This diagram shows Uranus in its orbit around the Sun.

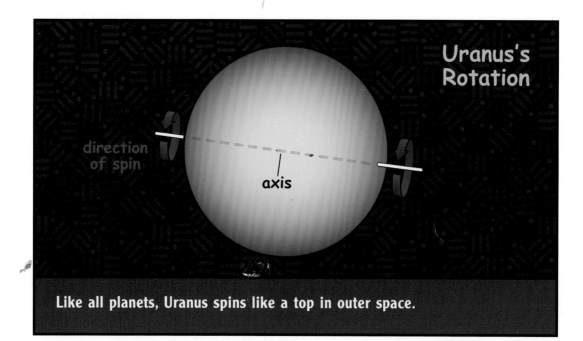

direction
of spin

axis

Like all planets, Uranus spins like a top in outer space.

A year is the time it takes for a planet to orbit the Sun. An Earth year is 365 days. But it takes Uranus much longer to circle the Sun. A year on Uranus lasts 84 Earth years.

Uranus and the planets also rotate (ROH-tayt). To rotate is to spin around like a toy top. All planets rotate around an axis (AK-suhs). An axis is an imaginary line that runs through a planet. The axis goes in one end of the planet and out the other. Those two ends are called the poles.

The side of Uranus that faces away from the Sun is in its night.

A day is the time a planet takes to rotate all the way around. Gas giants rotate faster than the rocky planets. A day on Earth lasts 24 hours. A day on Uranus lasts about 17 Earth hours.

The axis of a planet is usually pointed up and down. Or it is tilted just a little. But Uranus is tilted completely sideways. Long ago, a large object the size of a planet might have crashed into Uranus. The crash might have tipped the planet over.

Uranus moves through space on its side.

The sideways tilt of Uranus means that one of its poles is always facing the Sun. For half the year on Uranus, the north pole points toward the Sun. That means daylight at that pole lasts all that time—42 Earth years. Meanwhile, the south pole is in darkness for 42 Earth years.

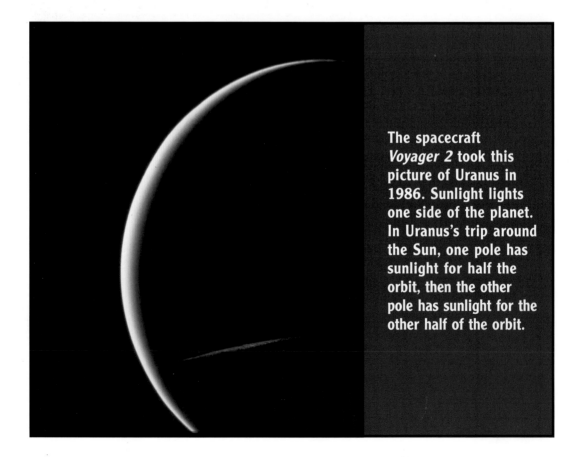

The spacecraft *Voyager 2* took this picture of Uranus in 1986. Sunlight lights one side of the planet. In Uranus's trip around the Sun, one pole has sunlight for half the orbit, then the other pole has sunlight for the other half of the orbit.

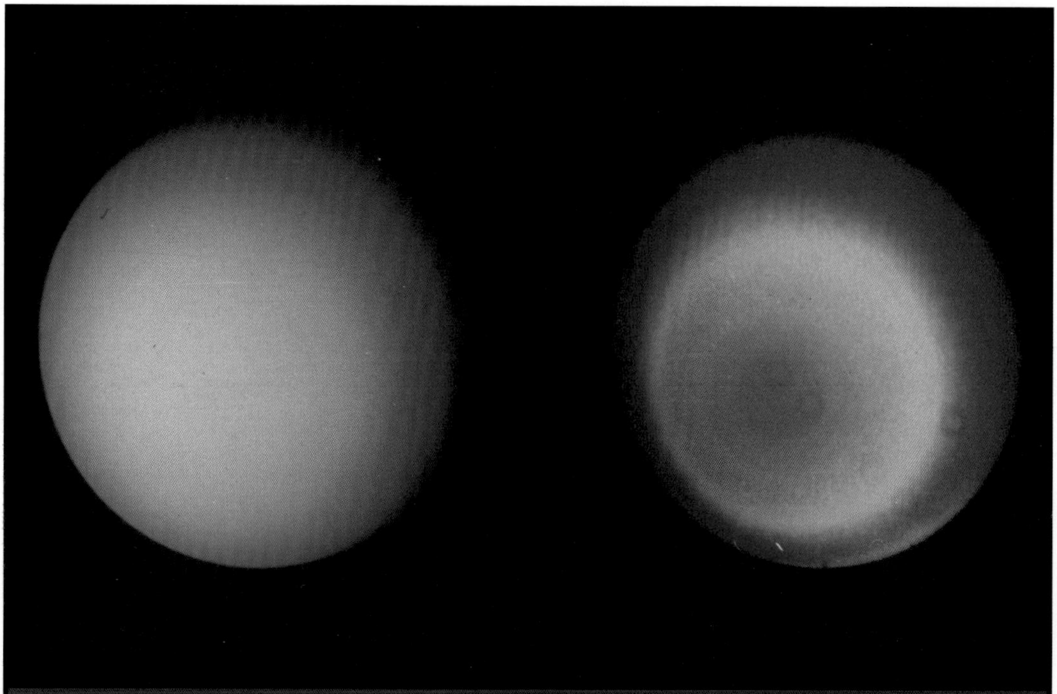

This picture shows two views of Uranus's south pole as it orbits facing the Sun. The picture on the left shows the planet as it would appear to human eyes. The picture on the right was taken with special cameras that show the hottest part of the planet in red.

Then, as Uranus orbits, the south pole faces the Sun. It will be daylight there for 42 Earth years. And the north pole will be in darkness.

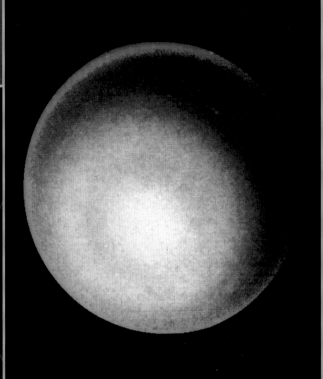

Uranus looks like a foggy blue ball. Is Uranus's air like Earth's?

CHAPTER 3
MYSTERIOUS GAS GIANT

At first, astronomers thought Uranus was boring. It didn't have big stripes and spots as Jupiter has. It didn't have Saturn's wide rings. But a closer look showed scientists that Uranus

Humans have never visited Uranus because it is so far from Earth. But imagine that you could visit. You'd have to hold your breath. The air is poisonous. Dress warm too. The temperature is –357°F (–216°C). The record coldest temperature on Earth is only –128°F (–89°C). Finally, hold on to your hat. In some places, the wind blows 450 miles (724 km) per hour.

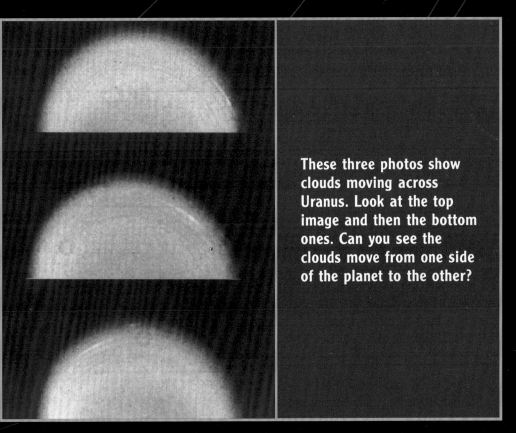

These three photos show clouds moving across Uranus. Look at the top image and then the bottom ones. Can you see the clouds move from one side of the planet to the other?

Uranus is surrounded by a layer of gases. The layer is called an atmosphere (AT-muhs-feer).

Clouds form high in Uranus's atmosphere. The sunlight hits these frozen clouds and reflects back through a gas called methane. This gives the planet its blue green color.

Methane is the gas that gives Uranus its blue color. Methane also exists on Earth. It gives natural gas stoves their blue flames.

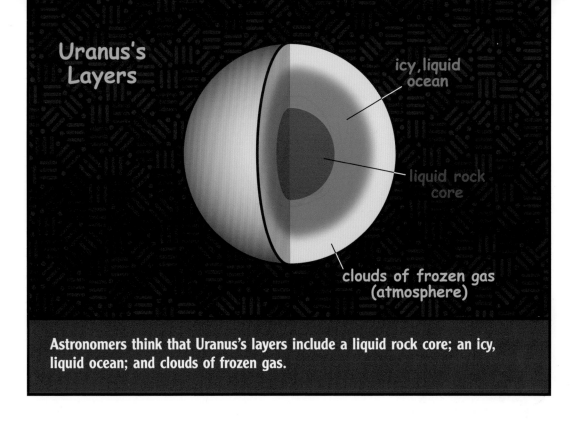

Uranus's Layers

icy, liquid ocean

liquid rock core

clouds of frozen gas (atmosphere)

Astronomers think that Uranus's layers include a liquid rock core; an icy, liquid ocean; and clouds of frozen gas.

There are more cloud layers deeper in the atmosphere. These clouds are probably made of water droplets. Under the clouds is an icy, liquid ocean.

Beneath the ocean, at the center of the planet, is the core. Scientists think the core is a ball of liquid rock. It may be about the size of Earth. Inside the core, the temperature rises to 9,000°F (5,000°C).

Uranus is huge! If you were to stand on the moon closest to the planet, Uranus would seem to fill the sky.

Uranus is huge compared to Earth. Sixty-three Earths could fit inside Uranus. But Uranus only weighs as much as 14 Earths. Earth is mostly rock. That makes it very heavy for its size.

Astronomers carefully study Uranus. In 1977, they were waiting for the planet to pass in front of something. What was it?

CHAPTER 4

RINGS AND MOONS

In 1977, astronomers made an exciting discovery. The astronomers were watching Uranus move around the Sun. They knew that the planet would pass in front of a distant star.

The starlight would shine through Uranus's atmosphere. Such an event was a great time to watch Uranus. The extra light would help astronomers learn about the far-off planet's atmosphere. They knew it would shine through the atmosphere, not through the planet.

These four astronomers from Cornell University in Ithaca, New York, were excited to have the chance to study Uranus's atmosphere in 1977.

The astronomers used a telescope on a airplane called the Kuiper Airborne Observatory (ABOVE) to study Uranus. The airplane belongs to NASA. It was equipped with special instruments.

Uranus began passing in front of the star. But then the astronomers saw something strange. The starlight blinked on and off five times before it even got to Uranus's atmosphere.

The planet passed by the star. Then, on the other side, the starlight blinked five more times. What was going on?

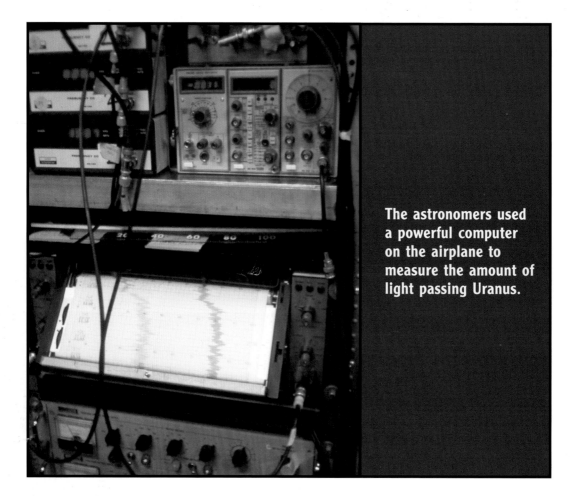

The astronomers used a powerful computer on the airplane to measure the amount of light passing Uranus.

Something near Uranus was blocking the star's light. It was making the star look like it was blinking. The astronomers discovered that Uranus has five narrow rings. The rings were too thin and too faint to be seen from Earth. But they were thick enough to block the star's light.

Since then, astronomers have found six more rings. The closest ring is 10,000 miles (16,000 km) from the planet. The farthest is 60,000 miles (97,000 km) from Uranus. A couple of the rings are several thousand miles wide and about 300 feet (90 meters) thick.

Uranus's widest rings are some of the farthest from the planet's surface. This picture has been specially colored to show the rings more clearly.

But most of the rings are very narrow. They are just a few miles wide. The rings are made of bits of dust, rock, and ice. The outermost ring is made of ice boulders that are several feet or meters across.

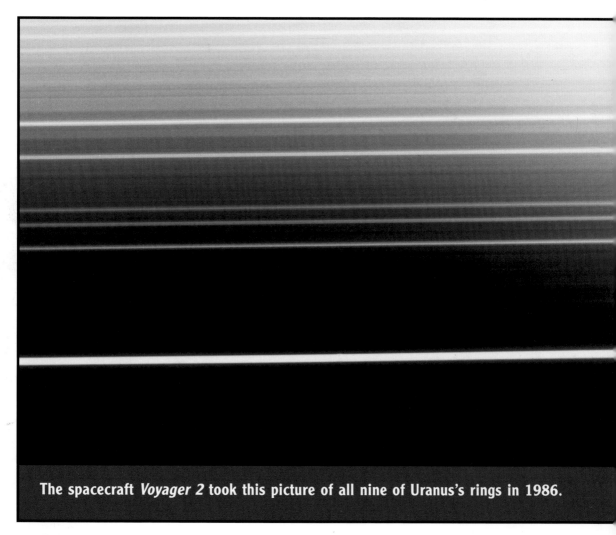

The spacecraft *Voyager 2* took this picture of all nine of Uranus's rings in 1986.

Rings aren't the only things near Uranus. Uranus also has at least 27 moons. Herschel discovered the largest moons in 1787. They are named Titania and Oberon. Astronomer Gerard Kuiper discovered the smallest moon, Miranda, in 1948.

Above: NASA photos show Uranus's five largest moons, from left to right: Miranda, Ariel, Umbriel, Titania, and Oberon. **Right:** Ten of Uranus's moons are visible in this photograph. It was taken through a telescope.

From Earth, Uranus's moons appear as faint specks. Astronomers knew they were moons because they stayed with Uranus as it orbited the Sun. But what do they look like? What are they made of? Astronomers couldn't tell. Scientists would not learn more about the moons for many years.

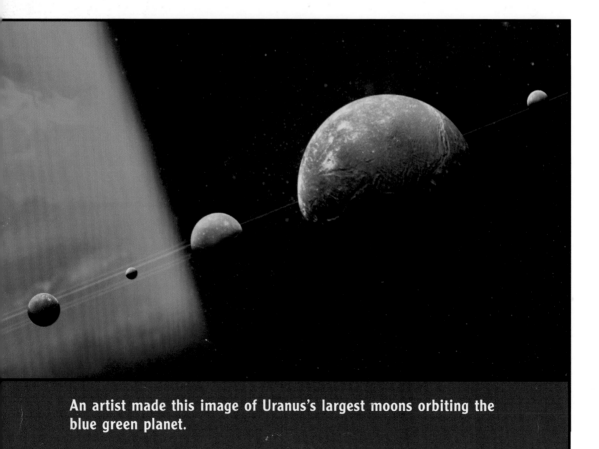

An artist made this image of Uranus's largest moons orbiting the blue green planet.

In this photograph taken through the Hubble Space Telescope, Uranus glows with reflected sunlight. Is the Sun very bright on Uranus?

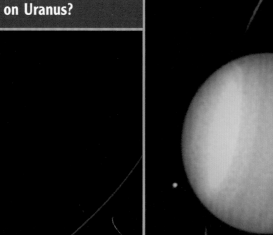

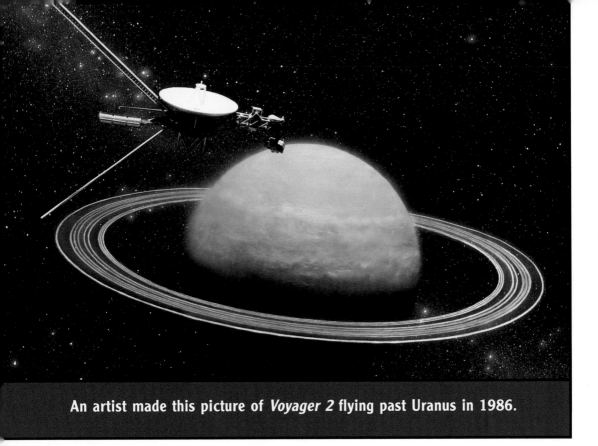

An artist made this picture of *Voyager 2* flying past Uranus in 1986.

In 1986 a spacecraft called *Voyager 2* sailed past Uranus. It was launched by the United States. *Voyager 2* took many pictures of Uranus. It sent the pictures back to Earth.

The spacecraft took images of Uranus's cloud tops, its rings, and its moons. With *Voyager 2,* scientists discovered two of Uranus's rings and ten more moons.

A few years later, the United States launched the Hubble Space Telescope (HST). The HST orbits above Earth. It aimed its powerful telescopes at stars and planets. It found more moons orbiting Uranus. Later, huge telescopes on Earth found more. By the 2000s, astronomers had found up to 27 moons around Uranus. They will probably discover more moons.

The Hubble Space Telescope floats in space above Earth.

Titania is Uranus's largest moon. It is not very big. Earth's moon is five times larger than Titania. Cordelia is one of the smallest moons and is the closest to the planet. It orbits Uranus at a distance of 15,000 miles (24,000 km). Tiny Ferdinand orbits almost 13 million miles (21 million km) away from the planet.

1986U3

1986U4

1986U1

ABOVE: *Voyager 2* took this picture of Titania in 1986. RIGHT: Astronomers discovered these three tiny moons around Uranus using pictures from *Voyager 2.*

Oberon is the moon farthest from Uranus's surface. It has more craters than any of Uranus's other moons.

All the moons have craters. Craters are deep, bowl-shaped dents on the surfaces of the moons. Craters are made when the moons are hit by meteorites (MEE-tee-uh-ryets). Meteorites are pieces of space rock or metal.

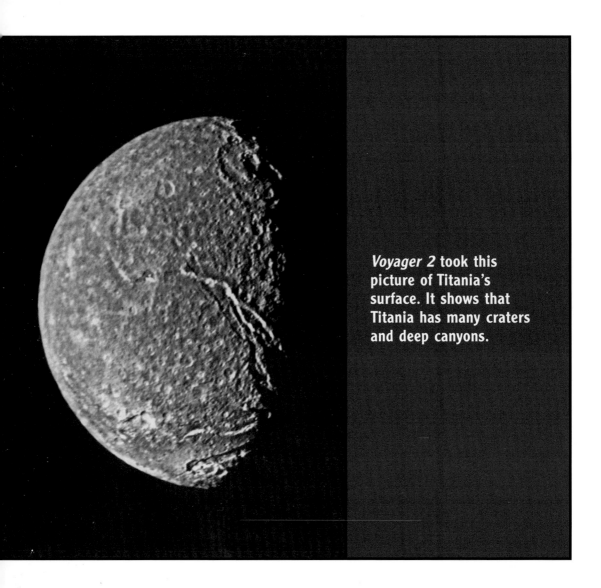

Voyager 2 **took this picture of Titania's surface. It shows that Titania has many craters and deep canyons.**

Titania is covered with small craters and rough rocks. Many cracks can be seen in its surface. Oberon has a mountain 4 miles (6 km) high.

The scientists' greatest surprise came from Miranda. Miranda has a canyon that is twelve times deeper than Earth's Grand Canyon. The canyon was made by a crack in the moon. Scientists think Miranda may have been struck by big space rocks several times. The moon broke and somehow came back together.

This picture from *Voyager 2* showed that the surface of Miranda is cracked and full of craters.

If you want to see Uranus, you first have to find out where it is. Sites on the Internet tell where each of the planets can be found in the night sky. Uranus will just look like a very faint star. With binoculars, you can see Uranus's blue green color. With a small telescope, Uranus will appear as a small dot.

If you look through a strong telescope, Uranus appears as a blue green dot. In this picture, Titania appears to the top left of the planet and Oberon appears to its bottom right.

Visitors to Uranus's moon Ariel might see Uranus rising over the horizon. An artist imagined this view.

In the 2000s, no scientists are planning spacecraft visits to Uranus. But that doesn't mean they aren't studying Uranus. We still have a lot to learn about this seventh planet from the Sun.

ON SHARING A BOOK

When you share a book with a child, you show that reading is important. To get the most out of the experience, read in a comfortable, quiet place. Turn off the television and limit other distractions, such as telephone calls. Be prepared to start slowly. Take turns reading parts of this book. Stop occasionally and discuss what you're reading. Talk about the photographs. If the child begins to lose interest, stop reading. When you pick up the book again, revisit the parts you have already read.

BE A VOCABULARY DETECTIVE

The word list on page 5 contains words that are important in understanding the topic of this book. Be word detectives and search for the words as you read the book together. Talk about what the words mean and how they are used in the sentence. Do any of these words have more than one meaning? You will find the words defined in a glossary on page 46.

WHAT ABOUT QUESTIONS?

Use questions to make sure the child understands the information in this book. Here are some suggestions:

> What did this paragraph tell us? What does this picture show? What do you think we'll learn about next? Is Uranus a planet or a star? When was Uranus discovered? How long does it take Uranus to travel around the Sun? What is Uranus made of? Does Uranus have moons? How do scientists study Uranus? Could humans visit Uranus? Why or why not?

If the child has questions, don't hesitate to respond with questions of your own, such as What do *you* think? Why? What is it that you don't know? If the child can't remember certain facts, turn to the index.

INTRODUCING THE INDEX

The index helps readers get information without searching throughout the whole book. Turn to the index on page 48. Choose an entry, such as *moons*, and ask the child to use the index to find out how many moons Uranus has. Repeat with as many entries as you like. Ask the child to point out the differences between an index and a glossary. (The index helps readers find information quickly, while the glossary tells readers what words mean.)

URANUS

BOOKS

Goldstein, Margaret J. *Our Solar System*. Minneapolis: Lerner Publications Company, 2003. Learn about the Sun, Uranus, and the other planets in this guide to our place in the universe.

Orme, Helen. *Let's Explore Uranus!* New York: Gareth Stevens, 2007. Launch into a trip to Uranus in this fun book.

WEBSITES

Extreme Space
http://solarsystem.nasa.gov/kids/index.cfm
The National Aeronautics and Space Administration (NASA) created this astronomy website just for kids.

HubbleSite
http://hubblesite.org/the_telescope/
This NASA website explains the Hubble Space Telescope's mission. The site includes photos, news, and a "Where's Hubble Now" interactive map.

NASA Science for Kids
http://nasascience.nasa.gov/kids
Readers will find lots of fun facts and activities about the solar system on this site.

Starry Night Sky Chart
http://www.space.com/snserver/snweb.php?zip=
Enter your zip code or map location to find out where the planets are in your night sky.

Uranus
http://kids.nineplanets.org/uranus.htm
This astronomy website offers lots of information about the seventh planet in our solar system.

GLOSSARY

astronomers (uh-STRAH-nuh-muhrs): scientists who study outer space

atmosphere (AT-muhs-feer): a layer of gases that surrounds a planet or moon

axis (AK-suhs): an imaginary line that runs through a planet. A planet spins on it axis.

elliptical (ih-LIHP-tih-cuhl): egg shaped

meteorites (MEE-tee-uh-ryets): pieces of space rock or metal

moons: small bodies of rock or ice that travel around planets

orbit: the path of a planet, moon, or other object in space around the Sun or a planet. *Orbit* can also mean to move along this path.

rings: particles of dust, rock, and ice that circle a planet and look solid from a distance

rotate (ROH-tayt): to spin around like a top

solar system: a group of planets and other objects that travel around the Sun

spacecraft: a machine with or without people that travels from Earth to outer space

telescope (TEH-luh-skohp): an instrument that makes faraway objects appear bigger and closer

INDEX

Pages listed in **bold** type refer to photographs.

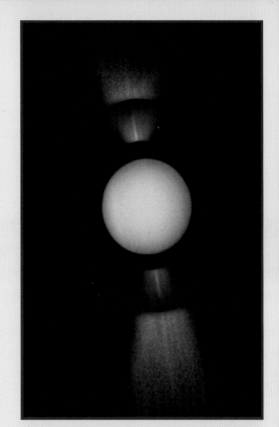

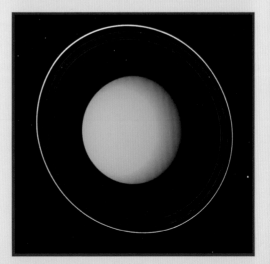